Contents

Introduction

Welcome to the *Cambridge IGCSE™ and O Level Computer Science Computer Systems Workbook*. This and the companion *Algorithms, Programming and Logic Workbook* replace the previous *Computer Science Workbook* and are designed to complement the second edition of the Student's Book and support the Cambridge IGCSE, IGCSE (9-1) and O Level Computer Science syllabuses (0478/0984/2210).

The aim of this Workbook is to provide you with further opportunity to practise the skills and test the knowledge and understanding you have acquired through using the first six chapters of the *Cambridge IGCSE and O Level Computer Science Second Edition* Student's Book. It is designed as a 'write-in' book to supplement your learning of different topics as you work through each chapter of the Student's Book and can be used either for home study or in class. The Workbook is intended to be sufficiently flexible to suit whatever you feel is the best approach according to your needs.

The chapters in this Workbook have the same names as those in the Student's Book and reflect the theory topics in the Student's Book.

1 Data representation

1 Convert the denary number 165 into:

a binary

....

....

b hexadecimal

....

....

....

2 a Convert the following binary number into denary:

0 1 1 1 0 1 1 0

....

....

b Convert the following hexadecimal number into denary:

5F

....

....

c Convert the following binary number into hexadecimal:

1 0 1 0 1 1 0 0 0 1 0 0

....

....

d Convert the following hexadecimal number into binary:

3ED

....

....

....

3 a How many mebibytes (MiB) of storage would be needed to store 800 photographs each of which are 16 MiB in size?

....

....

....

b Write your answer from part **a** in gibibytes (GiB).

....

....

4 The ASCII code for 'A' is 65 and for 'a' is 97.

a Write these denary values in 8-bit binary:

i 65

....

....

ii 97

....

....

b State the denary ASCII code for 'V' and 'v'.

i 'V'

....

....

  ii 'v'

....

....

 c Write the two denary values in part **b** in 8-bit binary format:

  i 'V'

....

....

  ii 'v'

....

....

 d Using your answers to part **a** and part **b**, suggest an easy way of finding the ASCII binary code for a lower-case letter (for example, 'm') if the ASCII code for the upper-case letter (for example, 'M') is known.

....

....

....

....

5 A computer system uses binary codes for letters of the alphabet as follows:

A = 10, B = 11, C = 12, ... , X = 33, Y = 34, Z = 35

 a Write the denary value for 'X' in binary using an 8-bit register:

 b To convert the binary code for 'X' to the binary code for 'x', all the bits in the 8-bit register in part **a** undergo a logic shift **two** places to the left.

  i Write down the contents of the 8-bit register after the bits, representing 'X', have been moved two places to the left.

    ii Convert the binary value in part **b i** into denary:

....

....

c State the denary values for the following two letters using the method described in part **b**.

    i r:

....

....

....

    ii m:

....

....

....

6 a Convert the denary number 4 4 8 0 1 into hexadecimal.

....

....

b Convert the hexadecimal number in part **a** into a 16-bit binary number.

....

....

7 State **three** uses of the hexadecimal system.

    1 ....

....

    2 ....

....

    3 ....

....

8 Six questions are shown on the left and eight numerical values are shown on the right.

Draw lines to connect each question to its correct numerical value (two of the numerical values are not used).

What is the denary value of this hexadecimal digit? E	10
What is the denary value of this binary number? 0 0 0 1 1 1 0 0	12
	14
If the download speed for broadband is 8 mebibytes per second, how long would it take to download a 96 mebibyte file (in seconds)?	16
	22
If $2x$ = 1 tebibyte (TiB), what is the value of x?	28
What is the hexadecimal value of this denary number? 50	32
How many bits are there in two bytes of data?	40

9

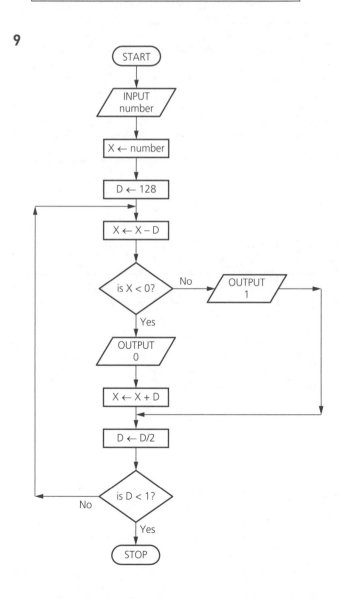

a Trace through the flowchart using the following two values as inputs:

i 220

Number	X	D	OUTPUT

ii 73

Number	X	D	OUTPUT

b Explain the function of the flowchart in part **a**.

....

....

10 a i Convert 0 1 0 1 1 1 1 0 into denary.

....

....

ii Convert 0 0 1 1 1 1 0 1 into denary.

....

....

b i Add together 0 1 0 1 1 1 1 0 and 0 0 1 1 1 1 0 1, giving your answer in binary.

....

....

....

ii Convert your answer in part **b i** to denary.

....

....

....

11 a Write down the largest number that can be represented by the following binary register.

Give your answer in binary and denary form:

128	64	32	16	8	4	2	1

....

....

b i Add together 0 1 1 1 0 1 1 1 and 1 0 0 1 1 1 0 1, giving your answer as an 8-bit binary number.

....

....

....

....

ii Comment on your answer to part **b i**.

....

....

....

....

12 An 8-bit binary register contains the following value:

0	0	1	1	1	1	0	0

a Write down the denary value of the register.

....

....

b The contents of the register undergo a logical shift one place to the right.

i Show the result of this right shift:

ii Write down the denary value of your answer to part **b i**.

....

....

iii The register in part **b i** now undergoes a further logical shift two places to the right. Comment on your result.

....

....

....

....

....

....

c The content of the original register (shown in part **a**) now undergoes a logical shift **two** places to the left.

i Show the contents of the register after this left shift operation.

ii State, with reasons, the effect of this shift on the denary value shown in part **a**.

....

....

....

....

13 a Convert the denary numbers, 37 and 19, into 8-bit binary numbers:

37: ....

19: ....

b Add together the two binary numbers in part **a**, and give your answer in binary.

....

....

....

....

c Carry out a logical shift, **two** places to the left, on your result from part **b**.

Comment on your answer.

....

....

....

....

d Carry out a logical shift, **four** places to the right, on your result from part **b**.

Comment on your answer.

....

....

....

....

14 A computer system uses two's complement notation.

a Complete the headings for an 8-bit binary number which uses two's complement:

64   32   16   8   4   2   1

....

b Write down **i** the **most negative** and **ii** the **most positive** numbers that can be stored in an 8-bit register which uses two's complement. Give your answers in both denary and binary format.

i most negative:

denary value:

....

....

   ii most positive:

   denary value:

....

....

c Convert the following two denary numbers into 8-bit binary numbers which use the two's complement format.

   i +47

   ii −59

d Convert the following two binary numbers, written in two's complement format, into denary.

   i 1 1 0 0 1 1 1 0

....

....

   ii 1 1 1 1 1 1 1 0

....

....

e **i** Convert the denary number, +45, into binary, using the two's complement format.

....

   ii Convert the denary number, −45, into binary, using the two's complement format.

....

....

iii Add together the binary numbers found in parts **e i** and **e ii**, leaving your answer in binary. Comment on the result.

....

....

....

....

....

....

15 a A camera detector has an array of 4096 by 2048 pixels and uses a colour depth of 16.

Calculate the size of an image taken by this camera; give your answer in MiB.

....

....

....

....

....

....

....

b An audio CD uses 40960 samples per second, with 16 bits being used per sample.

The music being sampled uses two channels to allow for stereo recordings.

Calculate the file size for a 1024 second recording. Give your answer in MiB.

....

....

....

....

....

....

....

16 a Give **three** reasons why it is often necessary to reduce the size of a file.

1 ....

....

....

2 ....

....

....

3 ....

....

....

b Explain the difference between lossy and lossless file compression.

....

....

....

....

....

....

....

c i Give **one** example of the use of lossy file compression.

....

....

ii Give **one** example of the use of lossless file compression.

....

....

17 In terms of representing bitmap images, explain the following:

a colour depth: ....

....

....

....

b image resolution: ....

....

....

....

18 Explain the difference between ASCII code and Unicode.

....

....

....

....

....

19 Seven statements are shown on the left and eleven computing terms are shown on the right in the diagram below.

Draw lines to connect each statement to the correct computer term.

In a binary number, this is the right-most binary digit	Overflow error
Method used by a computer to allow the representation of negative numbers as well as positive numbers	Resolution
	Unicode
Result of adding two binary numbers that exceeds the maximum size of a number which can be stored	American standard code for information interchange
The moving of bits to the left or to the right in a register, which represents multiplication by 2^x or division by 2^x (where x represents the number of places the bits are moved left or right)	Pixel
	Two's complement
A 7-bit code used to represent letters, numbers and characters found on a standard keyboard plus 32 control codes	Sampling rate
	Logical shift
Number of sound samples taken per second when representing sound digitally in a computer	Least significant bit
	Error code
The smallest element of a picture	Colour depth

20 a Which one of the following is not a correct hexadecimal number?

    A CODE

    B AX1S

    C 1DEA

    D FACE

  b The number of bits used to represent a sound sample is known as:

    A the sampling rate

    B amplitude value

    C loudness of a sound sample

    D sampling resolution

c The MP3 format removes redundant sound from a file. Which one of the following best describes the type of file reduction being used by the MP3 format?

A lossy files compression

B sound file damping

C image file compression

D lossless file compression

d Temporary files produced by a camera where no compression has been applied, are called:

A jpeg files

B png files

C gif files

D raw bitmap files

e Lossless file compression, which reduces the size of a string of adjacent, identical data, is called:

A jpeg

B run-length encoding

C sampling resolution

D audio compression

21 a Explain what is meant by run-length encoding (RLE).

....

....

....

....

....

....

....

b

i The above monochrome image is being designed.

Each white square is represented by 'W' and each dark square is represented by 'D'. Show how run-length encoding (RLE) would be used to produce a condensed file for the above image. Using the grid below, write down the data you would expect to find in the RLE compressed format; the first two have been done for you.

3W	2D								

ii Assuming that each square in the 8 × 8 grid requires one byte of storage, and each character in the RLE code also requires one byte of storage (for example, '3' requires 1 byte, 'W' requires 1 byte), calculate the file size reduction when using RLE.

....

....

....

....

22 a Explain the following terms used in the electronic storage of sound:

i sampling resolution:

....

....

....

ii sampling rate:

....

....

....

b Look at the sound wave below that has been sampled:

Sample number

<-------------1 second------------- × -------------1 second------------->

i   From the graph, what is the sampling resolution?

....

....

ii From the graph, what is the sampling rate?

....

....

iii Using the *x*-axis, locate points 9 and 18 on the graph. Write down the 4-bit binary values corresponding to the *y*-axis values of these two points.

point 9:				
point 18:				

c Discuss the benefits and drawbacks of increasing the sampling rate and sampling resolution when representing sound in an electronic (binary) format.

....

....

....

....

....

....

23 Write down a series of steps that could be used to convert a denary number into a hexadecimal number. Your steps should allow somebody to follow them clearly to give the correct converted value.

....

....

....

....

....

....

....

....

....

....

....

24a State what is meant by a bit.

....

b Give two reasons why computers use binary numbers rather than decimal numbers.

1 ....

....

....

2 ....

....

....

c Explain why the hexadecimal number system is used by computer technicians and programmers.

....

....

....

....

....

....

....

....

2 Data transmission

1 a Explain the term data packet.

....

....

....

....

....

....

....

....

....

....

....

....

b Data packets contain a header. Name **three** components that you would expect to find in a header.

1 ....

2 ....

3 ....

c Data packets also have a payload and a trailer. Explain these two terms.

payload: ....

....

....

trailer: ....

....

....

d

i Using the above diagram, explain how packet switching works when sending a 500 KiB file from computer 'A' to computer 'B'.

....

....

....

....

....

....

ii Using the diagram, explain why data packets need to be reassembled at computer 'B'.

....

....

....

....

2 Packet switching is used to send packets of data over a network.

a Give **three** benefits of using packet switching.

1 ....

....

....

2 ....

....

....

3 ....

....

....

b Give **three** disadvantages of using packet switching.

1 ....

....

....

2 ....

....

....

3 ....

....

....

c Data packets can get lost due to 'bouncing' around from router to router and never reaching their destination.

Explain the problems caused by data packets 'bouncing'.

....

....

....

3 a Data transmission depends on data direction and how many bits of data can be sent at a time. Complete the table below to show what type of data transmission is being described in each case. Tick (✓) two boxes for each description.

Description of transmission taking place	Simplex (✓)	Half-duplex (✓)	Full-duplex (✓)	Serial (✓)	Parallel (✓)
Data sent one bit at a time down a single wire in one direction only					
Data sent 16 bits at a time down 16 wires in both directions, but not at the same time					
Data sent 16 bits at a time down 16 wires in both directions simultaneously					
Data sent 8 bits at a time down 8 wires in one direction only					
Data sent one bit at a time down a single wire in both directions simultaneously					
Data sent one bit at a time down a single wire in both directions, but not at the same time					

b Five statements about serial and parallel data transmission are made in the table below. By placing a tick (✓) in the appropriate column, select which statements refer to serial transmission and which statements refer to parallel transmission.

Statements	Serial (✓)	Parallel (✓)
Transmission method used by the memory bus inside a computer		
Data can be skewed (out of synch) when travelling over long distances		
Least expensive of the two types due to fewer hardware requirements		
Most appropriate if data is time-sensitive; for example, when live streaming where faster transmission rate is essential		
Suffers from less risk of external interference		

4 a Explain what happens when a device is plugged into a computer using one of the USB ports.

....

....

....

....

....

....

b Seven statements about USB connections are made in the table below. By ticking (✓) the appropriate box, indicate which statements are true and which statements are FALSE.

Statements	True (✓)	False (✓)
USB uses a protocol that allows for error-free data transmission between device and computer		
USB can support any cable length between device and computer		
USB uses serial data transfer		
USB connections can transfer data using half-duplex or full-duplex		
It is difficult to add more USB ports to a computer using USB hubs		
USB data transfer rates are much faster than, for example, Ethernet connections		
There is no need for devices to have a power source because USB cable supplies 5V of power		

5 a A system uses even parity. Indicate whether the following bytes would fail or pass an even parity check:

1	1	0	0	0	0	1	1

....

1	0	1	1	0	1	1	0

....

0	0	0	1	1	1	1	1

....

b Explain why parity checks are used.

....

....

c Nine bytes of data were transmitted from one computer to another computer. Even parity was used by both systems. An additional byte, called the parity byte was also sent at the end of the transmission.

The following table shows the nine bytes and parity byte following transmission.

	Parity bit	Bit 2	Bit 3	Bit 4	Bit 5	Bit 6	Bit 7	Bit 8
Byte 1	1	1	1	0	1	1	1	0
Byte 2	1	0	0	0	0	1	0	0
Byte 3	0	1	1	1	0	0	1	0
Byte 4	0	1	1	1	1	0	1	1
Byte 5	1	1	0	0	0	1	1	0
Byte 6	0	1	1	0	1	1	0	1
Byte 7	1	0	0	1	0	0	0	0
Byte 8	0	1	1	1	1	1	0	1
Byte 9	0	0	0	0	1	0	0	1
Parity byte:	0	0	1	1	1	1	0	0

i One of the bits has been transmitted incorrectly. Indicate which bit is incorrect by giving its bit number and byte number:

bit number: ....

byte number: ....

ii Explain how you arrived at your answer to part **c i**.

....

....

....

....

....

....

iii Write down the corrected byte.

....

iv Describe a situation where a parity check wouldn't identify which bit had been transmitted incorrectly.

....

....

....

....

v Name and briefly describe another method to check if data has been transmitted correctly.

....

....

....

....

6 a Explain how the checksum system is used to identify any errors during data transmission.

....

....

....

....

....

....

....

....

b Explain how echo checks are used to check data following data transmission.

....

....

....

....

c Explain how automatic repeat requests (ARQs) work during data transmission.

....

....

....

....

....

....

....

....

7 Check digits are used to check data during data entry.

a Give **four** types of error that check digits can identify.

1 ....

....

2 ....

....

3 ....

....

4 ....

....

b ISBN-13 is a type of check digit standard.

   i The following algorithm generates a check digit for a 12-digit ISBN book code:

      1 add all odd-numbered digits together

      2 add all even-numbered digits together and then multiply the result by 3

      3 add together the results for steps 1 and 2, and then divide the result by 10

      4 take away the remainder of the division from 10, leaving the check digit

      Showing your working, calculate the check digit for the following 12-digit ISBN code:

      9 781 471 86867

ii The following algorithm checks that the check digit in a 13-digit code is correct:

1 add all odd-numbered digits together, including the check digit

2 add all even-numbered digits together and then multiply the result by 3

3 add together the results for steps 1 and 2, and then divide the result by 10

4 the check digit is correct if the remainder is zero

Showing your working, use the above algorithm to check whether or not the check digit in the following ISBN-13 code is correct:

9 781 471 80721 8

....

....

....

....

....

....

....

8 For each of the following ten questions, choose which of the five options corresponds to the correct response.

a What is meant by the term ciphertext when used in encryption? Circle the correct answer.

A an encryption or decryption algorithm

B a message before it has been encrypted

C a type of session key

D another name for plaintext

E text following an encryption algorithm

b Which one of the following statements about asymmetric encryption is true? Circle the correct answer.

A uses a public key only

B uses both a public key and a private key

C always uses 64-bit encryption

D the value of the private key is symmetrical

E uses private key only

c In encryption, which of the following is the term used to describe the message before it is encrypted? Circle the correct answer.

A simpletext

B plaintext

C notext

D ciphertext

E firsttext

d Which of the following is the biggest disadvantage of using symmetric encryption? Circle the correct answer.

A it is very complex and time consuming

B it is rarely used anymore

C the value of the key reads the same in both directions

D it only works on computers with older operating systems

E there is a security problem when transmitting the encryption key

e Which of the following is the correct name for a form of encryption in which both the sender and the recipient use the same key to encrypt and decrypt? Circle the correct answer.

A symmetric key encryption

B asymmetric key encryption

C public key encryption

D same key encryption

E block cipher encryption

f Which of the following is the final number in a code, calculated from all the numbers in the code, whose purpose is to find errors in data entry? Circle the correct answer.

A parity check

B checksum

C cyclic redundancy check

D parity bit

E check digit

g Which of the following is a form of error detection that makes use of a system of acknowledgements and timeouts? Circle the correct answer.

A automatic repeat request

B echo check

C check digit

D parity bit

E cyclic redundancy check

h Which of the following methods uses an extra bit added to a byte to ensure it contains an even number of 1s or odd number of 1s? Circle the correct answer.

A cyclic redundancy check

B parity check

C checksum

D check digit

E echo check

i Which of the following uses a calculated value which is sent after a block of data: the receiving computer also calculates the value from the block of data and compares the values? Circle the correct answer.

A parity check

B check digit

C packet switching

D checksum

E automatic repeat request

j Which of the following describes the check where the receiving computer sends back a copy of the data to the sending computer to allow it to compare the data? Circle the correct answer.

    A echo check

    B automatic repeat request

    C checksum

    D parity check

    E check digit

9 Some students sat a computer science exam. A number of their responses were incorrect.

Explain why the following eight responses given by the students are incorrect:

a 'A data packet header contains the MAC address of the sending computer and the receiving computer.'

....

....

....

....

b 'Half-duplex refers to the fact that four bits of data (half a byte) can be sent from "A" to "B" along four single wires.'

....

....

....

....

c 'Because USB connections can be fitted in any way, they have become the industry standard.'

....

....

....

....

d 'Odd parity means a binary number has an odd value, for example, 01110001 (i.e. 113).'

....

....

....

....

e 'Even parity means a binary number has an even number of zeros.'

....

....

....

....

f 'Check digits are used to make sure data has been transmitted without errors.'

....

....

....

....

g 'A checksum is calculated by adding up all the 1-bits in a byte, and sending this value at the end of the byte.'

....

....

....

....

h 'Asymmetric encryption makes use of the same key to encrypt and decrypt an encoded message.'

....

....

....

....

10 Five statements are shown on the left and eight computer terms are shown on the right in the following diagram.

Draw lines to connect each statement to the correct computer term.

Error checking method where data is sent to another device and is then sent back to the sender; if the two sets of data are different then there has been an error during transmission	Symmetric encryption
	Encryption
Data is made unreadable to anyone without the necessary keys to unlock the encoded data	Cipher text
	Echo check
A form of encryption which makes use of a public key and a private key to encrypt and decrypt coded messages	Full-duplex
Transmission error check that makes use of positive acknowledgement and timeout following data transmission	Asymmetric encryption
	Half-duplex
Type of data transmission where data can be sent in both directions at the same time	Automatic repeat request

11 Use the following word/phrase list to complete the paragraph below. Each word or phrase may be used once, more than once or not at all.

» algorithm	» decrypt	» matching pairs	» private
» asymmetric encryption	» document	» matching private	» public
» cipher text	» encrypted	» mathematically	» public key
» confidential	» matching document	» plain text	» symmetric encryption

.... makes use of a .... key and a .... key. Suppose Asif and Karl both work for the same company, and Asif wants to send a confidential .... to Karl.

Asif and Karl's computers both use the same .... to generate their own .... of keys; these keys are .... linked, but cannot be derived from each other. Karl now sends his .... to Asif. Asif now uses Karl's .... to encrypt the document he wishes to send to Karl.

Asif then sends his .... document back to Karl. Karl uses his .... key to unlock Asif's .... and .... it.

3 Hardware

1 The diagram shows a typical fetch-decode-execute cycle. However, five of the stages have been omitted. Complete the fetch-decode-execute diagram using the following stages. Write the **number** of the stage **only** in the diagram.

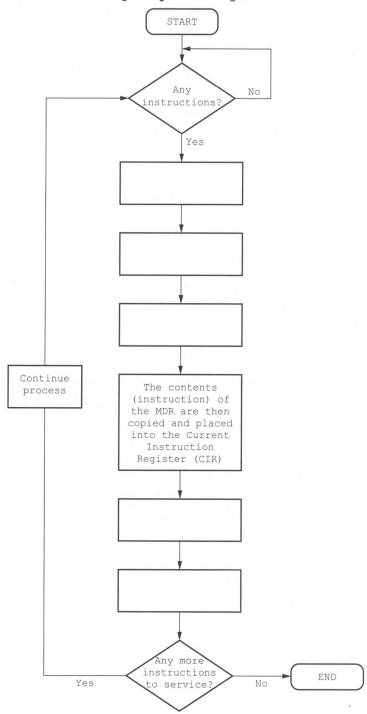

Stage	Description of stage
1	Address is then copied from the program counter (PC) to the memory address register (MAR) via the address bus
2	Contents of memory location contained in MAR are then copied into MDR
3	Instruction is decoded and then executed by sending out signals via the control bus to the computer components
4	The PC contains the address of the memory location of the next instruction to be fetched
5	Value of the PC is incremented by 1 so it now points to the next instruction to be fetched

2 a Name **three** types of bus used in the von Neumann architecture.

....

....

....

b The contents at a number of addresses are shown below.

Address	Contents
1000 0000	0111 1100
1000 0001	1000 0011
1000 0010	1111 1101
1000 0011	0111 1110
1000 0100	1100 1101
↓	↓
1111 1100	
1111 1101	0110 0011
1111 1110	1010 0111
1111 1111	1111 0011

i Show the contents of the MAR and MDR if we READ the contents of memory location 1 1 1 1 1 1 1 0.

MAR:								

MDR:								

ii Show the contents of the MAR and MDR if we wish to write 1 1 0 0 1 1 0 1 into memory location 1 0 0 0 0 1 0 0.

MAR:								

MDR:								

iii If MAR contains 1 1 1 1 1 1 0 0 and MDR contains 0 0 1 1 1 1 0 0, complete the memory contents diagram above.

c Four registers are shown in the following table. For each register, give its full name and explain its function in the fetch-decode-execute cycle.

Register	Full name of register	Function of register
CIR		
MAR		
MDR		
PC		

3 a Explain the meaning of the following terms, with reference to the CPU.

i (system) clock cycle: ....

....

....

ii cache: ....

....

....

b Discuss how changes to the clock speed and to the number of cores can affect the performance of the CPU. Include any advantages and disadvantages, due to these changes, in your discussion.

....

....

....

....

....

....

....

4 a i Define what is meant by an embedded system.

....

....

....

....

ii State **four** of the features you would expect to find in any embedded system.

1 ....

....

....

2 ....

....

....

3 ....

....

....

4 ....

....

....

iii Describe **three** applications that use embedded systems.

1 ....

....

....

2 ....

....

....

3 ....

....

....

b A games console is controlled by an embedded system in the form of a microcontroller. New games are supplied on a memory stick or via an internet connection. Various devices, such as a steering wheel, are connected to the console.

i Describe the inputs needed by the embedded system and describe what outputs you would expect to be produced. You may find it helpful to draw a diagram of your system.

....

....

....

....

....

....

....

ii Updates to the internal software in the games console are required every six months. Explain how the device software is updated without the need to send the games console back to the manufacturer every six months.

....

....

....

....

5

a A barcode showing three digits, A, B and C, is shown above. Each dark bar represents a 1-value and each light bar represents a 0-value.

Give the 7-bit binary value for each of the three digits.

A ....

B ....

C ....

b A supermarket uses barcodes on all its items. When a customer goes to checkout, a number of input and output devices may be used.

Name two input devices and two output devices. Give a different use for each named device.

input device 1: ....

use: ....

....

input device 2: ....

use: ....

....

output device 1: ....

use: ....

....

output device 2: ....

use: ....

....

c Give **two** benefits to the supermarket manager and **two** benefits to customers of using barcodes on all items.

Manager

1 ....

....

2 ....

....

Customer

1 ....

....

2 ....

....

6 A camera uses an embedded system.

a Name **three** of the tasks controlled by the embedded system in the camera.

1 ....

2 ....

3 ....

b Name **two** applications where a digital camera could be used.

1 ....

....

2 ....

....

7 Choose the most suitable input device for each of the following applications. A different device must be given in each case.

Application	Most suitable input device
Entering text and numbers into a word processor or spreadsheet	
Selecting an option or icon from an on-screen menu	
Inputting a user's voice into a computer as part of a voice recognition system	
Converting a hard copy document into an electronic form to be stored in a computer	
Reading a QR code using a smartphone or tablet	
Keying in digits from a barcode which did not scan correctly	
Reading data directly from the surroundings, such as taking a temperature	

8 Mobile phone touch screens can use three different types of touchscreen technology:
- capacitive
- infrared
- resistive

In the following table, give the advantages and disadvantages of all three types of touchscreen technology, when compared to each other.

Touch screen technology	Advantages	Disadvantages
Capacitive		
Infrared		
Resistive		

9 a Give **three** advantages of using digital light projectors when compared to LCD projectors.

1 ....

....

....

2 ....

....

....

3 ....

....

....

b Give **two** disadvantages of using digital light projectors when compared to LCD projectors.

1 ....

....

....

2 ....

....

....

10 Inkjet printers and laser printers are used in many offices.

a Give **one** advantage and **one** disadvantage of each type of printer when compared to each other.

Inkjet printer:

Advantage: ....

....

....

Disadvantage: ....

....

Laser printer:

Advantage:...

....

....

Disadvantage: ....

....

....

b Three tasks are given below. For each task, name the most suitable type of printer and give a reason for your choice.

   i Printing 20 000 colour leaflets to advertise a new pizza shop.

     Printer: ....

     Reason for choice: ....

     ....

     ....

   ii Printing a single high gloss photograph in colour.

     Printer: ....

     Reason for choice: ....

     ....

     ....

   iii Printing out physical replicas of coins for sale in a museum shop.

     Printer: ....

     Reason for choice: ....

     ....

     ....

11 a A car enthusiast has bought a car made in 1921. Unfortunately, none of the parts for the car are still made.

Explain how 3D technology could be used to create any part for this car.

....

....

....

....

....

....

b Describe **three** other uses of 3D printers.

1 ....

....

....

2 ....

....

....

3 ....

....

....

12 Eight types of sensor are shown on the left and eight potential sensor applications on the right.

Draw lines to connect each sensor to an appropriate application. Only one application can be assigned to each sensor.

Level sensor	Control/monitor the amount of water in the soil in a greenhouse
Moisture sensor	Used by a mobile phone to change between portrait and landscape modes
Light sensor	Monitor the amount of fuel in a car's petrol tank
Infrared (active) sensor	Turn on the windscreen wipers automatically when rain is detected
Pressure sensor	Used in the anti-lock braking systems in an aeroplane under-carriage
Acoustic sensor	Switch vehicle headlights on or off automatically
Magnetic field sensor	Measuring the weight of a lorry or van at a weigh station
Accelerometer	Pick up the noise of breaking glass in a security system

13 A security system uses three different types of sensor to detect intruders.

a Name **three** types of sensor that could be used.

1 ....

2 ....

3 ....

b Describe how the sensors and microprocessor are used in the security system. The output is the operation of a siren and flashing lights if an intruder is detected.

....

....

....

....

....

....

....

14 a Explain the differences between primary memory and secondary storage.

....

....

....

....

....

....

b In the following table, tick (✓) which description refers to RAM and which refers to ROM.

Description	RAM (✓)	ROM (✓)
Temporary memory device		
Non-volatile memory		
Data stored in this memory cannot be altered		
Permanent memory device		
Stores data and part of the operating system currently in use		
Can be increased in size to improve the operational speed of a computer		

c A model radio-controlled car contains RAM, ROM and also has a USB connection. The operation of the car is controlled by a remote control which communicates using radio waves.

i State what data or information would be stored on the ROM chip.

....

....

....

....

ii State what data or information would be stored on the RAM chip.

....

....

....

....

iii Explain why a USB port has also been included in the model car.

....

....

....

....

15 Backing storage makes use of magnetic, optical or solid-state technology.

Seven descriptions are given in the table below. Indicate with a tick (✓) which statements refer to magnetic, optical or solid-state technology.

Description	Technology used		
	Magnetic (✓)	Optical (✓)	Solid state (✓)
Makes use of floating gate and control gate technology			
Disk surfaces are made up of tracks and sectors; storage relies on certain properties of the iron oxide coating			
Devices using this technology have no moving parts			
Data is stored in 'pits' and 'lands' on a single spiral track running from the centre outwards			
Disks use the properties of laser light to allow read and write operations			
Data is stored by controlling the movement of electrons within NAND chips			
This technology is affected by strong magnetic and radio fields			

16 There are ten statements in the table below. Indicate, using a tick (✓) whether each statement is true or false.

Statement	True (✓)	False (✓)
Devices using magnetic media have a very slow data transfer rate		
HDD platters can be made from ceramic, glass or aluminium coated in iron oxide		
HDD surfaces are split up into tracks and sectors		
HDDs use a more reliable technology than solid-state devices, such as SSDs		
DVD-Rs are used to read and write data several times		
DVD and Blu-ray disks can both use dual-layer technology		
SSDs suffer from a high degree of latency		
Solid-state devices, known as flash drives, use NAND chip technology		
SSD data access time is approximately 100 times less than the data access time for HDDs		
Memory cards (such as the SD and XD cards used in cameras) are examples of magnetic media		

17 Describe how virtual memory works. In your description, include the benefits and drawbacks of virtual memory.

....

....

....

....

....

....

....

....

....

....

....

18 a Describe cloud (storage). Include in your description why this type of storage makes use of data redundancy.

....

....

....

....

....

....

....

b Describe the differences between public clouds, private clouds and hybrid clouds.

....

....

....

....

....

....

c i Describe **three** benefits of using cloud storage.

1 ....

....

....

2 ....

....

....

3 ....

....

....

ii Describe **two** drawbacks of using cloud storage.

1 ....

....

....

2 ....

....

....

19 Five computer terms are shown on the left and five descriptions on the right.

Draw lines to connect each computer term to its correct description.

Thrashing	Storage environment where the client and remote storage provider are different companies
Swap space	High rate of HDD read/write operations causing a large number of head movements
Cloud storage	Space on HDD or SSD reserved for data used in virtual memory management
Thrash point	Where an HDD is so busy doing read/write operations that execution of a process is halted
Public cloud	Method of data storage where data is stored on hundreds of off-site servers

20 a State which network terms are being described.

    i A circuit board or chip that allows a device to connect to a network:

    ....

    ii Type of address that uniquely identifies a device connected to a network:

    ....

    iii Address assigned by an ISP to a device each time it logs onto the internet:

    ....

    iv Hardware device that allows data packets to be moved between different networks:

    ....

    v Hardware or software that sits between a computer and an external network; it monitors traffic to and from the computer:

    ....

b i Explain what is meant by a dynamic IP address.

....

....

....

....

....

....

....

ii Describe **two** differences between a dynamic IP address and a static IP address.

....

....

....

....

....

c

i Complete the diagram using the terms:
- computer
- external network
- router
- switch

1 ....

2 ....

3 ....

4 ....

ii Describe the function of a router in a network.

....

....

....

....

....

....

....

21 When devices connect to the internet they are given IP addresses supplied by an ISP. IP addresses are necessary since the operation of the internet is based on a number of protocols.

a State what is meant by an ISP.

....

b State what is meant by a protocol.

....

....

c Two versions of IP addresses are called IPv4 and IPv6. Describe the differences between IPv4 and IPv6.

....

....

....

....

....

....

4 Software

1 Tick (✓) the appropriate column, in the following table, to indicate whether the named software is an example of system software or application software.

Software	System (✓)	Application (✓)
Photo editing software		
Graphics manipulation software		
Compiler		
Spreadsheet software		
Printer driver		
QR code reader		
Anti-virus software		
Screensaver		

2 a Give **three** of the general features of system software.

1 ....

....

2 ....

....

3 ....

....

b Give **three** of the general features of application software.

1 ....

....

2 ....

....

3 ....

....

c Give **three** examples of utility programs.

1 ....

....

2 ....

....

3 ....

....

3 Use the following list of words and phrases to complete the paragraph below.

Each word or phrase can be used once, more than once or not at all.

» anti-virus	» disk defragmenter	» infected	» security system
» background	» file compression	» locked	» smaller
» blocks	» file management	» quarantine	» tracks
» bootstrap	» head movements	» screensavers	» user
» contiguous	» heuristic checking	» sectors	» utility

Running .... software in the .... on a computer will constantly check

for virus attacks. Many .... utilities check software for certain behaviour which would

indicate a possible virus; this is known as .... Any possible files or programs which

are infected are put into .... until deleted by the .... or automatically

deleted.

As a hard disk drive (HDD) becomes full, ... used for data and files will become

scattered over different .... and .... on the disk surface. A ....

.... will rearrange the .... of data and files into ....

sectors wherever possible, thus reducing the scattering of data. It also reduces the number of HDD

....

Many computers use .... which automatically launch when a computer has

been inactive for a period of time. They form part of the ...., so that a user is

automatically logged out after a certain period of time and the .... will indicate that

the computer is now ....

4 a Write down **five** of the functions of a typical operating system.

1 ....

....

2 ....

....

3 ....

.... z

4 ....

....

5 ....

....

b The interface between a computer and a user is either a command line interface (CLI) or graphical user interface (GUI).

i Explain the terms CLI and GUI.

CLI: ....

....

GUI: ....

....

ii In the table below, six statements about interfaces are given. Tick (✓) the appropriate box to indicate whether each statement refers to a CLI or GUI interface.

Statement	CLI (✓)	GUI (✓)
The user is in direct communication with the computer		
The user is limited to the icons shown on the screen		
The user needs to learn a number of commands to carry out any operation		
Commands need to be typed in using the correct format and spelling		
There is no need for the user to learn any commands to use the interface		
The interface needs a complex operating system, such as *Windows*, to operate, which uses considerable amounts of memory		

5 Explain the function of each of the following in an operating system.

   a Multitasking management

   ....

   ....

   ....

   ....

   ....

   ....

   b Management of user accounts

   ....

   ....

   ....

   ....

   ....

   c Security management

   ....

   ....

   ....

   ....

   ....

6 a i Explain what is meant by an interrupt.

....

....

....

....

ii Give **three** examples of what can cause an interrupt.

1 ....

....

....

2 ....

....

....

3 ....

....

....

b i Explain what is meant by a buffer.

....

....

ii Explain why buffers are needed.

....

....

....

....

c The flowchart shows the use of interrupts and buffers when printing out a document. Some of the boxes in the flowchart are blank. Use each of the following statements to complete the flowchart. In each case, only write the number of the correct statement in the appropriate box.

1 Meanwhile, the processor is able to carry out other tasks while the (printer) buffer is being emptied.

2 Has all the data been sent to the printer?

3 The current task is suspended while the interrupt is serviced.

4 The contents of the (printer) buffer are emptied to the printer and the data from the document is printed.

5 When all the data has been printed, the (printer) buffer becomes empty; an interrupt signal is then sent to the processor requesting its attention.

6 Data from the document to be printed is sent to the (printer) buffer from the computer memory.

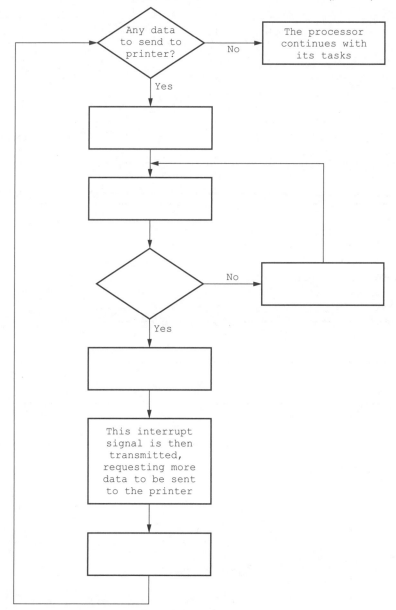

7 Memory management, security management and hardware management are three functions of an operating system. The following table shows eight statements. By ticking (✓) the appropriate box, indicate which statements refer to memory, security or hardware management.

Statement	Management type		
	Memory (✓)	Security (✓)	Hardware (✓)
Keeps a track of all memory locations			
Ensures that anti-virus software is regularly updated			
Prevents competing applications using the same memory locations at the same time			
Ensures that the appropriate device driver takes data from memory/file and translates it into a format the device can understand			
Management of devices to control the use of queues and buffers holding data temporarily			
Receives and handles error messages and interrupts from devices connected to the computer			
Manages RAM and allows data to be moved between RAM and devices, such as HDD or SSD			
Maintains access rights for all users of a computer system			

8 a Explain the function of a device driver.

....

....

....

....

b Explain the use of descriptors in a device driver.

....

....

....

....

   c Explain the role of a descriptor when a new device is plugged into a USB port of a computer for the first time.

....

....

....

....

9 a State what is meant by firmware.

....

   b Give two examples of firmware used in computer devices.

     1 ....

....

     2 ....

....

10 a State **three** benefits of writing a program in a high-level programming language.

     1 ....

....

     2 ....

....

     3 ....

....

   b Explain why a programmer would choose to write a program in a low-level programming language.

....

....

....

....

c Steve is writing a program to use his laptop to control the lighting system in his house. State, with reasons, which type of programming language would be most suitable for him to use.

Type of language: ....

Reasons: ....

....

....

11 Use the following list of words and phrases to complete the paragraph below.

Each word or phrase can be used once, more than once or not at all.

assembler	machine code
compilers	programmer
high-level	programs
interpreters	translates
language	translators

Programs written in a low-level .... are translated into .... by an ....

.... before they can be run on a computer. Programs written in a ....

.... are also translated into .... before they can be run on a computer.

There are two types of .... for .... languages .... and

....

12 a Describe the purpose of a compiler.

....

....

....

....

b Describe the purpose of an interpreter.

....

....

....

....

c Describe the purpose of an assembler.

....

....

....

....

13 A program is being developed in a high-level language. Both a compiler and an interpreter are being used for translation.

a i State when it is appropriate to use the compiler.

....

....

ii State when it is appropriate to use the interpreter.

....

....

b State **two** advantages of using an interpreter.

1 ....

....

2 ....

....

c State **two** advantages of using a compiler.

1 ....

....

2 ....

....

14 a Describe the purpose of an IDE.

....

....

....

....

b Error diagnostics is a feature of an IDE. Identify **three** other features of an IDE.

1 ....

....

2 ....

....

3 ....

....

c State the purpose of error diagnostics in an IDE. Give an example of its use.

....

....

....

....

5 The internet and cyber security

1 a Explain the fundamental differences between the internet and the world wide web (www).

....

....

....

....

....

....

....

A user typed in: **https://www.hoddereducation.com/comp_science_sample**

Identify:

i the protocol being used: ....

ii the domain host: ....

iii the domain type: ....

iv the file name: ....

c Describe **three** of the features of web browsers.

1 ....

....

2 ....

....

3 ....

....

2 A user wishes to locate a website so they can download some documents. The following sequence shows six steps in the location of the website and the download of the required documents. However, the sequence of steps shown is not in the correct order.

By writing the numbers 1 to 6, put each step in its correct order.

Order	Description of step
	The DNS server 1 cannot find the required website in its database or cache and sends out a request to DNS server 2
	The IP address is then sent back to the user's computer
	The computer now sets up a communication with the website server and the required pages are downloaded
	User opens their web browser and types in the URL; the web browser asks DNS server 1 for the IP address
	User's browser interprets HTML and displays the web pages on the user's computer
	DNS server 2 finds the URL and sends the IP address back to DNS server 1 which puts the IP address and URL into its database and cache

3 a Explain what is meant by a session cookie.

....

....

....

....

b Explain what is meant by a persistent cookie.

....

....

....

....

....

....

c Give **three** uses of cookies.

1 ....

....

2 ....

....

3 ....

....

4 a Indicate whether the following six statements about blockchaining are true or false by placing a tick (✓) in the correct box.

Blockchaining statement	True (✓)	False (✓)
All digital currency systems use blockchaining		
Blockchaining uses a decentralised database		
The last block in a blockchain is known as the 'genesis block'		
New hash values are only generated when data in a block is altered		
Tampering of data in a block by a hacker would cause the hash value to change		
Blocks are 'policed' by network users called 'miners'		

b When a new transaction in cryptocurrency takes place, a new block is created.

Name **three** values that would be created for this new block.

1 ....

....

2 ....

....

3 ....

....

c A blockchain has six blocks.

   i Complete the diagram below to show how the six blocks are connected to form a blockchain network. Use arrows to show any hash value links.

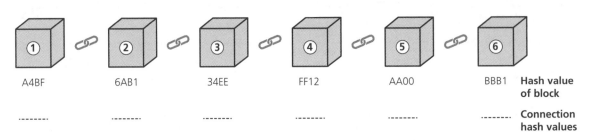

A4BF	6AB1	34EE	FF12	AA00	BBB1 **Hash value of block**
-------	-------	-------	-------	-------	------- **Connection hash values**

   ii Describe what happens if block '4' was hacked and the hash value was changed to DD22.

   ....

   ....

   ....

   ....

   ....

   ....

d Explain the difference between digital currency and cryptocurrency.

   ....

   ....

   ....

   ....

   ....

5 Eight security terms are shown on the left and eight descriptions are shown on the right in the following diagram.

Draw lines to connect each security term to its correct description.

Security term	Description
Brute force attack	Legitimate-looking emails sent out to users; once a link is clicked on, the user's web browser is sent to a fake website
Virus	Attempt at preventing users from accessing a website by flooding it with useless spam traffic which causes the website to become overloaded
Denial of service attack	A process that attempts to crack a password by systematically trying out all combinations of letters, numbers and symbols to find the password
Hacking	When a cybercriminal creates a situation that can lead to a potential victim dropping their guard and getting them to break normal security procedures
Worm	Malicious code installed on a user's computer or on a website; code redirects user's browser to a fake website without user's knowledge
Phishing	Program code that replicates with the intention of deleting or corrupting files; they need an active host to initiate the attack
Pharming	Malware that self-replicates; they do not need to target an active host program to initiate an attack
Social engineering	Act of gaining illegal access to a computer system without the owner's permission or knowledge

6 a Explain what is meant by the following **three** types of malware.

   i Trojan horse:

   ....

   ....

   ....

   ....

   ....

   ....

   ii Adware:

....

....

....

....

....

....

   iii Ransomware:

....

....

....

....

....

b **i** Explain what is meant by social engineering.

....

....

....

....

....

....

ii The following table contains four methods used by social engineering to target a victim. Complete the table by describing how each method is used. Include examples in your description.

Threat used by cybercriminals	How the threat is used (include examples)
Instant messaging	....
Scareware	....
Baiting	....
Phone calls	....

c Describe the steps taken by a cybercriminal when targeting their victim through social engineering.

....

....

....

....

7 a i Explain what is meant by anti-spyware.

....

....

....

....

ii Give **three** of the features of typical anti-spyware software.

1 ....

....

....

....

2 ....

....

....

....

3 ....

....

....

....

b Complete the table below to show the benefits and drawbacks of the **three** named biometric techniques.

Biometric technique	Benefits	Drawbacks
Fingerprint or thumbprint scans		
Retina scans		
Voice recognition		

c The diagram shows the use of voice control in a car. A microphone picks up the voice of the driver and carries out their commands. For added security, the system only responds to people authorised to drive the car.

Explain how the microphone and microprocessor are used to control the following functions using verbal input from the driver:
- operation of the satellite navigation system
- media (radio, streaming and telephone)
- security (window and door control).

....

....

....

....

....

....

....

....

....

....

....

....

....

8 a Brayan uses two-step verification when buying items from a website using his tablet. There are six stages in the two-step verification process. The stages are listed in the table below, but they are not written in the correct order. By writing the numbers 1 to 6, put each of the stages in their correct order.

Order of stage	Description of stage
	User takes note of the one-time authentication code (OTP)
	User enters the one-time authentication code into the tablet logged on to website
	User enters their website username and password on the tablet
	User is authenticated and allowed access to the website to make a purchase
	One-time authentication code is sent to user's registered smartphone
	Brayan registers his smartphone number on the website before using it to purchase any goods

b Explain the benefits to a user of allowing automatic updates to software on, for example, a smartphone.

....

....

....

....

9 One of the ways of checking the authenticity of emails and website links is to look out for spelling mistakes in the URL. Describe **four** other ways that can be used to identify potential fake emails and URL links. Include examples wherever possible in your answer.

....

....

....

....

....

....

....

....

....

....

....

....

....

....

10 a Explain what is meant by SSL.

....

....

....

....

b The table below shows what happens when a user wants to access a secure website and receive and send data.

The statements are not in the correct order. By writing the numbers 1 to 5, put each statement in its correct order.

Correct order	Statements
	The web browser then requests that the web server identifies itself
	If the web browser can authenticate the SSL certificate, it sends a message back to the web server to allow communication to begin
	The user's web browser sends a message requesting a connection with the required website which is secured by SSL encryption
	Once the message is received, the web server acknowledges the web browser, and the SSL-encrypted two-way data transfer can begin
	The web server responds by sending a copy of its SSL certificate to the users web browser

c Give **three** examples of where SSL would be used.

1 ....

....

2 ....

....

3 ....

....

11 a Explain why firewalls are used.

....

....

....

....

....

....

b Give **four** of the tasks carried out by a firewall.

1 ....

....

2 ....

....

3 ....

....

4 ....

....

6 Automated and emerging technologies

1 Use the following set of words or phrases to complete the paragraph below. Each word or phrase can be used once, more than once or not at all.

» attributes	» explanation system	» objects
» conclusions	» inference	» repository
» database	» inference engine	» rules base
» dialogue boxes	» inference rules	» search engine
» expert system	» knowledge base	» user interface

.... are a form of AI developed to mimic human knowledge and reasoning. They

use knowledge and .... to solve problems where a degree of human expertise

would be needed. Expert systems interact with the user by way of a .... through

.... and command prompts. Once a conclusion is found, the .... can

be used to inform the user of the reasoning behind the conclusion. The main processing element

of an expert system is the ...., which behaves like a search engine examining the

.... for data that matches the queries. The .... is the problem-solving

component which makes use of .... stored in the .... The knowledge

base is a collection of .... and their associated ....; it is often referred

to as a .... of facts.

2 Eight descriptions and ten computer terms are shown in the diagram below.

Draw lines to connect each description to the correct computer term.

Devices that can move between point 'A' and point 'B' without the need for manual input	Rules base
A form of AI that has been developed to mimic human knowledge and expertise	Knowledge base
Robots that roam the internet, scanning websites and categorising them for search purposes	Autonomous
Simulated intelligence in machines; building of machines capable of thinking like a human	Chat bot
A repository of facts and expertise in the form of a collection of objects and their attributes	Artificial intelligence
Combination of software and hardware designed and programmed to work automatically without the need of any human interaction	Expert system
A subset of AI in which the algorithms are 'trained' and can learn from their past experience and from examples	Robotics
Branch of computer science that brings together the design, construction and operation of 'intelligent' electromechanical machines	Machine learning
	Automated system
	Web crawler

3 Many examples of automated systems exist.

   a Define what is meant by an automated system.

....

....

....

....

   b One part of the automated system involves the use of sensors.

     Explain what a sensor is.

....

....

....

....

   c Name **three** areas where automated systems are used.

     1 ....

....

....

     2 ....

....

....

     3 ....

....

....

d Give **three** general advantages of using automated systems.

1 ....

....

....

2 ....

....

....

3 ....

....

....

e Give **three** general disadvantages of using automated systems.

1 ....

....

....

2 ....

....

....

3 ....

....

....

4   An example of an automated system is the control of the entry and exit to a private car park. Cameras take a photograph of a car's number plate on entry which is then checked before the barrier is raised. At the exit, another camera captures the car's number plate, which is again checked before raising the barrier.

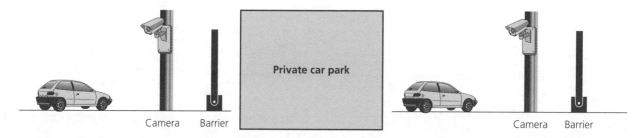

Camera   Barrier   Private car park   Camera   Barrier

a   Name the software that is needed to convert the camera image of the car's number plate into an electronic format that can be used in, for example, a database.

   ....

b   Describe how sensors, cameras, actuators and a computer system can be used to control entry to and exit from the car park. Your answer should include how a car number plate meets the criteria for entry and any other security or safety aspects.

   ....

   ....

   ....

   ....

   ....

   ....

   ....

   ....

   ....

   ....

   ....

   ....

c **i** Describe the advantages of using an automated system to control entry and exit to the car park.

....

....

....

....

ii One disadvantage is the possibility of illegal copying of number plates to 'fool' the system and allow unauthorised access to the car park.

Discuss how you might think this problem could be overcome.

....

....

....

....

5 **a** A car is equipped with self-parking technology. Explain the role of the following devices in the self-parking technology:

i cameras:

....

....

....

ii sensors:

....

....

....

iii actuators:

....

....

....

b Describe how embedded systems in a car prevent the driver exceeding a set speed and also prevent the car getting too close to the vehicle in front of it. Include the role of the microprocessor and any named sensors in your answer.

....

....

....

....

....

....

....

....

....

....

....

....

....

....

....

....

....

....

6 a Name suitable sensors for each of the following automated systems. Describe the function of your named sensor in each case.

Description of automated system	Suitable sensor(s)	Function of named sensors
Manufacture of a new vaccine which requires the mixing of four liquids in the ratio 1:2:3:4 as a single batch. The four liquids must be totally mixed and the temperature must be maintained at 35°C, which is critical to the process. When fully mixed, the solution turns an even yellow colour.	....	....
A lighting display has been set up in one room of an art gallery (as part of the exhibition). A random sequence of different coloured LED lights is under microprocessor control. The display only switches on when visitors walk into the room; at the same time, the room lights are dimmed to give the lighting display its most dramatic effect.	....	....
A train uses automatic twin-doors. Both doors open automatically when the train stops. Both doors close again when no-one is still boarding or leaving the train. The doors have a safety mechanism so that a passenger cannot become trapped between the two closing doors. The train can only move off when every door on the train has been safely closed.	....	....

b The eight statements on the left-hand side of the following table are either true or false. Tick (✓) the appropriate box to indicate which statements are true and which are false.

Statements	True (✓)	False (✓)
Automated systems lead to less consistent results or less consistent products		
Automated systems are more expensive to set up than traditional manual systems		
Automated systems could be quickly overwhelmed by the amount of data presented to them		
Automated systems are inherently less safe than manual systems		
Automated systems generally require enhanced maintenance when compared to manual systems		
Automated systems allow processes to run at optimum conditions at all times		
Software failures, due to unforeseen conditions, are unlikely to impact on an automated system		
Automated systems will react more quickly to unusual process conditions than a manual system		

7 a Complete the diagram of an expert system.

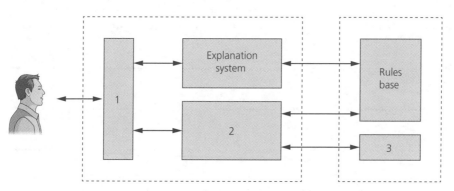

1 ....

2 ....

3 ....

b A section of a knowledge base is shown below.

	Attribute 1	Attribute 2	Attribute 3	Attribute 4
Bus	Hybrid electric/petrol engine	Uses a road	Has 4 wheels	Up to 80 passengers
Train	Electric motors	Uses rails	Has 40 wheels	Up to 400 passengers
Taxi cab	Diesel engine	Uses a road	Has 4 wheels	Up to 4 passengers

i What is the correct expert system name for the items in column 1?

....

ii The following set of questions was asked by the expert system. The user's answers to each question are shown. Using the knowledge base section shown above, what would be the expected output?

Expert system question	User response
Does it have a hybrid engine?	NO
Does it use a road?	YES
Does it have four wheels?	YES
Can it take more than 5 passengers?	NO

....

c Describe the steps in setting up an expert system.

....

....

....

....

....

....

....

....

8 a Explain what is meant by the following terms:

i artificial intelligence (AI):

....

....

....

....

ii machine learning:

....

....

....

....

b Describe the differences between AI and machine learning.

....

....

....

....

....

....

9 a Which one of the following is NOT a component of an expert system? Circle the correct answer.

A an inference engine

B rules base

C accelerometer

D knowledge base

E user interface

b The practice of getting a machine to make decisions without being programmed to do so, via data acquisition, is a feature of:

A robotics

B a search engine

C an inference engine

D an automated system

E machine learning

Circle the correct answer.

c The combination of software and hardware designed and programmed to work automatically without the need for human interaction is known as:

A a chatbot

B an automated system

C an expert system

D machine learning

E robotics

Circle the correct answer.

d The branch of computer science that brings together the design, construction and operation of electromechanical devices is known as:

A robotics

B control technology

C computer programming

D automated systems

E electronics

Circle the correct answer.

e Which one of the following is NOT an advantage to the management of using robots in an industrial application? Circle the correct answer.

A they can work 24/7 without the need for breaks or holidays

B their work is more consistent

C they lead to higher productivity

D they can cause deskilling of the workforce

E they are less likely to make errors